The Soul Afire

REVELATIONS
OF THE
MYSTICS

#

EDITED BY H. A. REINHOLD

PANTHEON BOOKS

COPYRIGHT 1944 BY PANTHEON BOOKS INC.
41 WASHINGTON SQUARE, NEW YORK 12, N. Y.

FIRST EDITION

NIHIL OBSTAT
ARTHUR J. SCANLAN, S.T.D.
Censor Librorum

IMPRIMATUR
FRANCIS J. SPELLMAN, D.D.
Archbishop, New York

DATE
October 9, 1944

MANUFACTURED IN THE UNITED STATES OF AMERICA
BY AMERICAN BOOK–STRATFORD PRESS, INC., NEW YORK

TO
JACQUES MARITAIN

CONTENTS

Introduction   xix

FIRST PART
THOU HAST MADE US FOR THEE

THE EROS OF THE INTELLECT

Logos spermatikos (*St. Augustine*)   3
The ascent from the underground den (*Plato*)   3
The winged soul (*Plato*)   4
The true Eros (*Plato*)   4
Our kindred are in Heaven (*Plato*)   5
The unknowing knowing of the Supreme Good (*Plotinus*)   6
Stripped to nakedness (*Plotinus*)   6
Flight of the alone to the Alone (*Plotinus*)   7
Unredeemed naturalism grasping for truth (*Plotinus*)   8
None but God's presence (*Rabindranath Tagore*)   9

THE WITNESS OF ISRAEL

Moses and the burning bush (*Exodus 3, 1-6*)   11
The cloud on the mountain (*Exodus 24, 16-18*)   11
The face of God (*Exodus 33, 9-11; 13-14; 18-23*)   12
The thrice Holy (*Isaias 6, 1-7*)   13
The Spirit entered into me (*Ezechiel 1, 4-6; 24-26; 28; 2, 1-2*)   13
The Word of the Ancient of Days (*Daniel 7, 9-10; 13-14*)   14

THOU ART A HIDDEN GOD

Introductory selections (*Bible, Léon Bloy, Dionysius the
Areopagite*)   16, 17

The blinded soul (*St. Anselm of Canterbury*) 17
God is All (*St. Gregory of Nyssa*) 18
God is wondrously above change (*St. Augustine*) 19
What is the divine darkness (*Dionysius the Areopagite*) 19
At best, God is seen only in shadows (*Cardinal Newman*) 21
Darkened by sin and dazzled by Thy light (*St. Anselm of Canterbury*) 22
The unspeakable majesty of God (*St. Augustine*) 23

KNOWING IN PART, DARKLY

Looking from afar (*Roman Breviary*) 25
Five apophthegms (*Angelus Silesius*) 26
We have not eyes keen enough (*Cardinal Newman*) 26
O depth of wisdom . . . (*St. Catherine of Genoa*) 27
From the life of St. Thomas Aquinas (*Jacques Maritain*) 28
From the life of St. Thomas Aquinas (*Peter Calo*) 28
A vision (*St. Hildegarde of Bingen*) 29
The desire to see God (*St. Hildegarde of Bingen*) 31
Reflection on a great mystery (*St. Brigid of Sweden*) 33

THE HEAVENS PROCLAIM THY GLORY

Introductory selections (*Bible, Dante*) 35, 36
Yea! Lord, whom I have not . . . (*Sir Lawrence Shipley*) 36
A canticle of Brother Sun (*St. Francis of Assisi*) 37
Episode of the fountain (*St. Gertrude of Helfta*) 38
Christian Platonism (*St. Augustine*) 39
God's Grandeur (*Gerard Manley Hopkins*) 40

THE RESTLESS HEART

Introductory selections (*Bible, Dante*) 41, 42
Thirsting heart (*St. Augustine*) 42
Thrusting towards the summit (*Dante*) 44
There is none good but One (*St. Augustine*) 45
The Collar (*George Herbert*) 46
For Him our hearts sigh (*Yves of Paris*) 47
The soul before God (*Cardinal Newman*) 48

THOU HAST MADE US FOR THEE, O GOD

Introductory selections (*Bible, Suso, Theologia Germanica, Lucie Christine*)   49, 50
Love is the nature of the soul (*St. Mechtild of Magdeburg*)   51
Of the true God (*St. Augustine*)   51
I would that I were home again ... (*Heinrich of Lauffenberg*)   53
Natural inclination to love God (*St. Francis de Sales*)   53
God intimately in us (*St. Thomas Aquinas*)   55
Our souls likened to the divine person (*St. Thomas Aquinas*)   55
Carrion Comfort (*Gerard Manley Hopkins*)   56

SECOND PART
ALL THINGS ARE BUT LOSS

DETACHMENT

Introductory selections (*Bible, Angelus Silesius*)   59
Alone with the Alone (*Symeon the Younger*)   59
Detachment (*Meister Eckhart*)   62
Diversities between nature and grace (*Imitatio Christi*)   67
Simplicity (*St. Francis de Sales*)   70
From the life of St. Thomas Aquinas (*Jacques Maritain*)   71
Be Thou my chooser for me (*Dame Gertrude More*)   71
The state of abandonment (*Father J. P. de Caussade*)   74

HOLY INDIFFERENCE

Introductory selections (*Bible, Dante, Blessed John Tauler, St. John of the Cross, William Faber*)   75, 76
Prayer of simplicity (*St. Jane Frances de Chantal*)   76
Repose in God (*St. Francis de Sales*)   77
Do not ask for or seek the free gifts of God (*St. Teresa of Avila*)   79
Three spiritual laws (*St. Francis de Sales*)   82
From the new song of inner freedom (*Anonymous*)   83
How could he grieve who beholds God? (*Anna of Munzigen*)   83

LABOURING PILGRIMS

Introductory selections (*St. John of the Cross, St. Hildegarde of Bingen, Pascal, St. Augustine*)   87

Why is it . . . (*Meister Eckhart*) 87
Spiritual labours of spring (*Blessed John Tauler*) 88
On the benefit of composure (*Meister Eckhart*) 93
On remoteness and on having God (*Meister Eckhart*) 94
How man can do his work (*Meister Eckhart*) 97
What man must do (*Meister Eckhart*) 98
How one should imitate God (*Meister Eckhart*) 100
Answer to a timid worker (*Meister Eckhart*) 102
Of spiritual aridity versus lukewarmness (*St. John of the Cross*) 105
To buy out time (*Father J. P. de Caussade*) 107
The prayer of one very ill (*Marguerite Teilhard de Chardin*) 109
The importance of patience (*Father Louis Lallemant*) 110
Aversions (*St. Francis de Sales*) 110

A BROKEN HEART THOU WILT NOT DESPISE

Introductory selections (*Bible, St. Bernard*) 111, 112
From a last will (*Blessed Angela of Foligno*) 112
Withhold Thy wrath (*Advent song*) 112
True sorrow (*St. Mechtild of Magdeburg*) 113
On the dignity of temporal suffering (*Suso*) 113
On excess of penance (*Richard Rolle*) 115
The lukewarm penitents (*William Faber*) 115
God writes straight on crooked lines (*St. Augustine*) 116
The gentle Lord (*Bossuet*) 117
O felix culpa (*Roman Missal*) 117

THE FLESH, ERROR AND SIN

Introductory selections (*Bible*) 118
The two sides of religion (*Cardinal Newman*) 118
The hostile body (*St. Mechtild of Magdeburg*) 119
All flesh is like grass (*St. John Chrysostom*) 120
The wisdom of this world is naught (*St. John of the Cross*) 121
Vanity (*St. Francis de Sales*) 123
A saint's horror of sin (*St. Catherine of Genoa*) 124
It is I who heal (*Pascal*) 124
God's scourge in our sins (*Meister Eckhart*) 126
Error disguises itself as truth (*St. Augustine*) 126
Acedia, or spiritual tedium (*Cassian*) 128
The right understanding of evil (*St. Augustine*) 130
St. Catherine of Genoa (*Jean de Menasce*) 132

Dies Irae (*Thomas a Celano*)   133
Litanies (*John Donne*)   135
The Day of Wrath (*St. Columba*)   136

LAW AND FREEDOM

Introductory selections (*Bible*)   137-139
Our blindness to freedom (*Father Joseph Le Clerc du
    Tremblay*)   139
Pride and false freedom (*Theologia Germanica*)   140
Some things are for use (*St. Augustine*)   142
Difference between use and enjoyment (*St. Augustine*) 143
Trinity true object of enjoyment (*St. Augustine*)   143
Spiritual adulthood (*St. John of the Cross*)   144

ALL THINGS ARE BUT LOSS

Introductory selections (*Bible*)   145
The curing fever of love (*St. Macarius the Egyptian*) 146
A soul drawn to God (*St. Ignatius Loyola*)   147
Hunger and thirst (*St. Macarius the Egyptian*)   148
Our entire being must be freed (*St. Gregory of Nyssa*) 149
The trap of mediocrity (*Father J. J. Surin*)   150
On spiritual poverty (*Meister Eckhart*)   152
Prayer for the true things (*Roman Missal*)   153
But one thing is needful (*Book of the Poor in Spirit*) 153
A prayer (*Richard Rolle*)   154
What do I love (*St. Augustine*)   155

THIRD PART

APPREHENDED BY JESUS CHRIST

THE MYSTICAL BODY

Introductory selections (*Bible, St. Thomas Aquinas,
    St. Augustine, St. Bernard*)   159-161
A Litany (*John Donne*)   162
Verily, God has no need . . . (*Meister Eckhart*)   162
If, while the mouth prays . . . (*St. Francis de Sales*) 162
We are tempted to believe . . . (*Fénelon*)   162
Blessed City, Jerusalem (*Monastic Breviary*)   162

Now I recognise what the Church is . . . (*Anna Katharina Emmerich*)   163

Antiphon for Holy Thursday (*Roman Missal*)   164

Membership in God (*St. Augustine*)   164

The Preface of Pentecost (*Roman Missal*)   165

A vision of the Church (*St. Hildegarde of Bingen*)   165

Te Deum (*Roman Breviary*)   166

Blessing during the Eucharist (*Roman Missal*)   168

Love your neighbour (*St. Augustine*)   169

THE NEW CREATION: OUR CONVERSATION IS IN HEAVEN

Introductory selections (*Bible*)   170-171

God be in my head (*Anonymous*)   172

Even if all teachers . . . (*Blessed John Tauler*)   172

The composed "I" . . . (*Suso*)   172

Who desires to understand . . . (*Imitatio Christi*)   172

I shall place the candle . . . (*St. Mechtild of Magdeburg*)   172

Do not show your inner reverence . . . (*St. Teresa of Avila*)   172

The crown of the new creation (*St. Juliana of Norwich*)   173

Letter to a nun recently clothed (*Suso*)   173

The invisible kingdom (*Cardinal Newman*)   175

The simplicity of the righteous is derided (*St. Gregory the Great*)   176

Already we see through the mist (*St. Gregory the Great*)   177

There are people . . . (*Meister Eckhart*)   177

All in God (*Charles Péguy*)   178

The birth of the eternal Word (*Meister Eckhart*)   178

True knowledge is a principle of love (*Don Luigi Sturzo*)   181

The fire of divine love (*St. Frances of Rome*)   182

Hymn to Christ (*Clement of Alexandria*)   183

THE TWO WAYS: MARTHA AND MARY

Introductory selections (*Bible*)   184

On the two ways (*St. Augustine*)   184

Martha's service (*St. Augustine*)   185

The more perfect must be humble (*The Cloud of Unknowing*)   188

The two callings (*Blessed John Tauler*)   189

The gulf between God and us (*Cardinal Newman*)   192

A modern Mary (*Lucie Christine*)   192

EUCHARISTIA

Introductory selections (*Bible*) 195
The Slain Lamb (*The Armenian Liturgy*) 195
Eucharistic prayer (*Didache*) 198
Prayer (*St. Bonaventure*) 199
Transformed into Christ's body (*Luis de Leon*) 199
Long hunger wasted the world wanderer (*Radbod*) 201
Come and taste (*St. Gregory the Great*) 201
The holy sign of unity (*St. Augustine*) 202
Adoro Te devote (*St. Thomas Aquinas*) 203
The altar is Christ (*St. John Chrysostom*) 204
The bread of mystery (*St. Augustine*) 204
Easter Sunday (*Sedulius Scottus*) 205

NOT HAVING OUR OWN RIGHTEOUSNESS

Introductory selections (*Bible*) 206
In God's mighty hand (*St. Teresa of Avila*) 207
Be more trusting in God (*St. John of the Cross*) 208
Make yourselves little (*Cardinal Newman*) 210
Humility of the intellect (*Imitatio Christi*) 211
Elevation in humility (*Blessed Angela of Foligno*) 212

CONFORMABLE UNTO HIS DEATH

Introductory selections (*Bible*) 213-214
The Beloved and the Lover (*Ramon Lull*) 214
The symbolism of the crucifixion (*St. Gregory of Nyssa*) 215
Let me become the wheat of Christ (*St. Ignatius of Antioch*) 215
St. Francis of Assisi and Christ (*Fioretti*) 216
Mortification (*Cassian*) 219
You fill up the full measure of Christ's passion (*St. Augustine*) 219
The extraordinary road (*St. Mechtild of Magdeburg*) 220
Conformable unto His death (*Cardinal Newman*) 220
Soul of Christ, sanctify me! (*Anonymous*) 221
The Cross meaneth . . . (*Suso*) 222
Many souls . . . (*Lucie Christine*) 222
I had the deep feeling . . . (*Léon Bloy*) 222

FOURTH PART

THE CLOUD OF UNKNOWING

THE STILL SMALL VOICE

Introductory selections (*Bible, Hippolytus of Rome*)   225, 226
Eternal birth (*Meister Eckhart*)   226
How the Word of God speaks unto the heart (*St. Augustine*)   226
The token of true calling (*The Cloud of Unknowing*)   227
Spiritual frailty (*St. Jane Frances de Chantal*)   228
The kind hand that sustains all the world (*Yves of Paris*)   229
Hymn to the Paedagogus (*Clement of Alexandria*)   229
Prayer of love (*St. Augustine*)   230

THE LOVING PURSUER

Introductory selections (*Bible, Meister Eckhart, St. Bernard*)   231, 232
The love of God (*St. Augustine*)   232
God's love seeks us out (*St. Augustine*)   232
God's lovableness (*Suso*)   234
The embrace (*Hugh of St. Victor*)   238
The soul and God (*St. Mechtild of Magdeburg*)   239
Jesu, nostra redemptio (*Monastic Breviary*)   240

THE CLEANSING

Three apophthegms (*Angelus Silesius*)   242
O God, break the tyranny . . . (*Cardinal Newman*)   242
The stripping of Self (*St. John of the Cross*)   243
Empty thy heart (*Meister Eckhart*)   243
How God operates in man (*St. Isaac of Nineveh*)   244
The love of God in purgatory (*St. Catherine of Genoa*)   246
Living in Christ (*Theologia Germanica*)   247
Borne up by Christ (*St. Macarius the Egyptian*)   251

THE DARK NIGHT

Introductory selections (*Bible, Suso, St. Augustine, St. Thomas Aquinas*)   253-255
The song of the soul (*St. John of the Cross*)   255

The dark night of the spirit and of the senses (*St. John of the Cross*) 256
The cleansing fire of the dark night (*St. John of the Cross*) 258
God veils his mercy (*Anna Katharina Emmerich*) 261
Persistent prayer (*St. Teresa of Avila*) 263
The twofold way (*Meister Eckhart*) 264

THE WOUNDED HEART

Introductory selections (*Bible*) 266, 267
Song of love (*Richard Rolle*) 267
Vision of an angel (*St. Teresa of Avila*) 268
The knowledge and savour of love (*St. Mechtild of Magdeburg*) 269
An ecstatic confession (*St. Catherine of Siena*) 270
Mutuality of love (*St. Catherine of Siena*) 273
Christ's wounds are all open (*The Nun's Rule*) 273
Wounded by flame in God (*St. John of the Cross*) 274

THE BRIDE

Introductory selections (*Bible, Ramon Lull, Fénelon*) 276-278
Description of his own mystical experiences (*St. Bernard*) 278
A Peruvian saint's experience (*St. Rose of Lima*) 280
Six songs of love (*St. Mechtild of Magdeburg*) 281
The knight and his celestial Lady (*Father Léonce de Grandmaison*) 285
Loving madness (*St. Maria Maddalena de' Pazzi*) 286
Consecration of virgins (*Roman Pontifical*) 287
Spiritual wedlock (*St. Maria Maddalena de' Pazzi*) 292
Mystical marriage (*St. Bernard*) 293

ECSTASIS: WORDS NO MAN CAN UTTER

Introductory selections (*Bible, St. Bernard*) 296, 297
Ecstasy (*St. Bernard*) 297
Memorial (*Pascal*) 299
Ecstasy (*Madame Acarie*) 300
Joined to God in the divine light (*Louis de Blois*) 301
As wood in a fire (*Luis de Leon*) 301
He and I are one (*Symeon the Younger*) 302
Language fails (*St. Catherine of Genoa*) 304

Praying in a transport of mind (*Cassian*)   304
One must hunt down one's nature (*Father Joseph Le Clerc du Tremblay*)   305
Sentiments of love (*Father Lyonnard*)   306
Shapeless beauty (*Marie Tessonier*)   307

SOBRIA EBRIETAS: THE GREAT SILENCE

Introductory selections (*Monastic Breviary, Bible*)   308, 309
Praise of God (*St. Mechtild of Magdeburg*)   310
The God of Darkness (*Blessed Angela of Foligno*)   310
I saw the Lord face to face (*St. Gertrude of Helfta*)   311
Wrestling with the blind naught (*The Cloud of Unknowing*)   312
All is merged (*Jean de Saint-Samson*)   313
God touches the soul immediately (*Blessed John Tauler*)   313
Chaste retirement of the loving soul (*Yves of Paris*)   316

THE LOVING GAZE

O sweet and delectable light (*Richard Rolle*)   318
From the beginning of time (*Gerlach Peters*)   319
Human nature purified reflects Divine Nature (*St. Gregory of Nyssa*)   320
The degrees of prayer seen by an early Eastern Saint (*St. Isaac of Nineveh*)   321
Adornment of spiritual marriage (*Blessed John Ruysbroeck*)   327
Degrees of prayer (*St. Teresa of Avila*)   334
On the prayer of recollection (*St. Teresa of Avila*)   345
The beginning of contemplation (*Father Louis Lallemant*)   350

CONCLUSION

INTO PARADISE

THE EXCELLENCE OF THE KNOWLEDGE OF OUR LORD

Introductory selections (*Bible, St. Anselm of Canterbury, St. Macarius the Egyptian, St. Bonaventure, Imitatio Christi*)   357, 358
Of the doctrine of truth (*Imitatio Christi*)   358
Can the soul foretaste eternal Blessedness (*Theologia Germanica*)   360

Experience at Manresa (*St. Ignatius Loyola*)   362
God's presence in the soul (*St. Teresa of Avila*)   363
The joy-giving perfection of God (*St. Catherine of Siena*) 363

THE CHANGING OF OUR VILE BODY

Introductory selections (*Bible, St. Francis de Sales, Lucie
  Christine, Suso, Yves of Paris, Paul Claudel*)   365-367
Losing ourselves in God (*St. Bernard*)   368
The end of the game (*St. Francis de Sales*)   369
You shall be unafraid in the face of death (*Suso*)   369
St. Francis' death (*St. Bonaventure*)   371
The death of Blessed Angela of Foligno (*Anonymous*)   373
Letter on his father's death (*Pascal*)   375
Conversation with Monica (*St. Augustine*)   376
A Christian is one of the everlasting company (*Cardinal
  Newman*)   378
The last cleansing (*St. Catherine of Siena*)   379
Epitaph (*Alcuin*)   381

HOLY, STRONG, IMMORTAL ONE

The heaven which so many lights (*Dante*)   383
God is a living God (*St. Thomas Aquinas*)   383
God's birth in us (*Meister Eckhart*)   385
The Son is born in us (*Blessed John Tauler*)   385
What is eternity? (*St. Augustine*)   391

IN PARADISUM DEDUCANT TO ANGELI

Introductory selections (*Roman Ritual, Bible*)   393, 394
The City of God (*St. Augustine*)   395
Is this the joy? (*St. Anselm of Canterbury*)   396
Like the bursting of a dyke (*Father J. J. Surin*)   397
Give God more than the dregs of life (*Yves of Paris*)   397
For all the long years . . . (*Cassian*)   398
St. Francis on perfect joy (*Fioretti*)   398
The face of God (*Nicholas of Cusa*)   400

On Scripture texts   402
Acknowledgements   403
Biographical Index   407